ccm *l i f e* L I N E S

Copyright © 2000 by CCM Books, a division of CCM Communications

Published by Harvest House Publishers, Eugene, Oregon 97402

Library of Congress Catalog-in-Publication Data
Hendrickson, Lucas
   ISBN 0-7369-0438-7

Printed in the United States of America

00 01 02 03 04 05 / IP / 10 9 8 7 6 5 4 3 2 1

Newsboys is managed by First Management Company, Nashville, Tennessee

A publication of CCM Creative Ventures · Writer: Lucas Hendrickson · Art direction and design: Mike Rapp, Gear/Nashville · Cover photograph: Michael Ru
   Interior photography: Various

NEWSBOYS

By Lucas W. Hendrickson

IN THE BEGINNING

What began as a lunchtime escape for some music-loving teenagers in Mooloolaba, in the state of Queensland in Australia, has become one of the hardest working forces in pop music today.

Those restless teenagers brought not only their friends into their adventure, but eventually, millions of fans from all around the world.

NEWSBOYS

Today, the Newsboys have all the confidence that would befit a pop band at the top of its game, but all the while infused with the humble spirit found only in members constantly striving to be men of God.

The Newsboys have been through everything you could imagine a band going through, and then some. Members coming and going. Critical acclaim in some corners, critical skewering from others. Young guys just moved to America from Down Under living on a dollar a day, to wizened veterans playing in front of tens of thousands of people a night.

Today, the Newsboys is a vastly different unit than it was when lead singer Peter Furler first started searching out mates to jam with. Furler no longer plays with the guys he knew from grade school, but rather a fastidious former rival drummer from Queensland, a fast-talking New Zealander who chose bass playing over hairdressing, a keyboard-wielding kid from Detroit who had little-to-no idea what he was getting into that fateful night in Indianapolis, and a Polaroid-snapping guitarist from the Hoosier State who just wants to be seen as a normal guy.

And Furler wouldn't have it any other way.

The Newsboys of today is a band that's a hybrid of both its members and of their experiences together literally growing into adulthood under a spotlight and the occasional hydraulically-powered drum riser.

THE LONG ROAD AHEAD

It started out as a lot of musical legends do: Two guys get together and sort of say, "Let's put together a band." For Peter Furler, however, it took a little more convincing (and conniving) on his part.

"The original guitarist and I went to school together, and at lunch time, we used to jam to Beatles and Jimi Hendrix tunes, really whatever we could pull together the chords and beat for," Peter says. "There was a room that had a drum

kit, and George would bring his guitar, and there'd be an amp there, and we'd jam

"Take"-ing home the gold: In 1997, the Newsboys celebrated their first gold record, notching more than 500,000 units sold for *Take Me to Your Leader*.

on songs."

Apparently George Perdikas was fairly in demand as a guitar player in their

high school universe, as Furler had to rely on some creative accounting to rope him

into playing. "He was trying

> "I said I had a 10-piece drum kit, but
> what I had done was count all the pieces
> on the kit, not the drums themselves."
> - Peter Furler

to decide between two drum-

mers to jam with, and I told

him I had the bigger drum kit," Peter remembers. "I said I had a 10-piece drum kit,

but what I had done was count all the pieces on the kit, not the drums themselves.

He chose me, and that was sort of the start of it all."

Two other local lads, John James and Sean Taylor, were recruited to sing and play bass respectively, and the Newsboys were off and running. "It was really

formed out of the love for music, but a little bit of boredom too. We were in an

area where you didn't have huge malls and other things to distract your attention,"

Peter notes. "It wasn't even a case of 'What are we going to do with our lives?' —

> "It was really formed out of the love for music, but a little bit of boredom too."
> - Peter Furler

we just loved music and started playing.

"We played anywhere we could get an audience. We'd take the amps and the

drum kit down to the beach, we'd run the power from the public rest room, John would sing through George's amplifier, and we'd just put on a concert until the police told us to go away," Peter remembers. "On Friday and Saturday nights, we'd put a couple of guitars and some drumsticks in the trunk of the car and ride around looking for pubs where we could play. We'd show up somewhere, and when the band that was playing stopped to take a break, we'd ask if we could get up and play."

The relentless gigging caught the attention of promoters who were booking the Christian band WhiteHeart on their first Australian tour. The local heroes tore up that opening slot, so much so that three weeks after playing that fateful tour, the band was on a plane to New Jersey to make their first real record, *Read All*

NEWSBOYS

About It.

"We never really thought of coming over and playing in America as the primary goal. We never had that conversation," Peter says. "But we knew that if we kept playing the same places over and over in Australia, we'd definitely get burned out or wear out our welcome, whichever came first."

They didn't wear out their welcome in their homeland, that's for sure. When they returned home, new album in tow, the Newsboys were more in demand than ever, opening for artists such as Petra, Phil Keaggy, and Carman. But when they returned to the United States to give the American scene a go, the band found it a lot tougher than they ever imagined.

"When we first got here, there were a couple of guys in the band who had pretty high expectations, like we were going to come over here and immediately sell a million records," Peter remembers. "I was kinda on the other side, I just wanted to play music. I wanted to keep getting better at this craft.

...when they returned to the United States to give the American scene a go, the band found it a lot tougher than they ever imagined.

"Everyone got tired and burned out, and George decided to go home and get married. It was completely understandable, and it wasn't like there was a big brawl or anything. But it was tough. He went back, and we all went back as well. We hired another guitarist when we were back in Australia, a guy from New Zealand named Jonathan Geange. We came back to America and made *Hell Is for Wimps*."

Another record meant more touring. More touring meant another personnel change, adding Corey Pryor on keys. And another when Geange departed. More touring also meant time passed, and another album was needed, this one called *Boys Will Be Boyz*. But after their third album came out, and once again after a lot more touring, Furler knew something had to change.

"We moved to Nashville from Georgia, and I remember sitting in the first apartment I ever had and listening to the *Boys Will Be Boyz* album and just hating it. Just hating everything about it. I hated the lyrics, and I could say that because I wrote half of them," Peter recalls. "It was about that time that the president of Star Song hooked me up with Steve Taylor and we started working together. I wrote the music, and he wrote the lyrics.

"We were both looking around for a producer for this thing, but we were already cutting tracks and kinda running out of time. We got ready to mix and we were still looking for a producer, so we decided, 'Let's just co-produce this thing ourselves.'"

"This thing" was *Not Ashamed*, the record many saw as the Newsboys' first big breakthrough. "*Not Ashamed* really felt like our first record, the first one where it felt like we got the motorbike started. And that was the time we met Jody, and

Duncan and Jeff came in not long after that."

Jody was guitarist Jody Davis, Duncan was drummer (then keyboardist) Duncan

Phillips, and Jeff was keyboardist Jeff Frankenstein, joining Furler and James on

the road and remaining core members of the band. Bassist Kevin Mills signed up

> *Not Ashamed* really felt like our first record, the first one where it felt
> like we got the motorbike started. And that was the time we met Jody, and
> Duncan and Jeff came in not long after that.

for one tour of duty (and the album *Going Public*) after Taylor departed, and Phil

Joel filled Mills' shoes, where he remains to this day.

With this six-man core intact and Taylor once again behind the board, the

THE LONG ROAD AHEAD

Newsboys made their sixth album, *Take Me To Your Leader*, which showcased their increasing musical maturity while continuing their penchant for general wackiness.

Leader was a fun album, and touring it was a fun and ambitious enterprise, but at the end of it, John James hung up the shiny gold suit to pursue other interests, namely spending time with his family.

James' departure, along with the remaining members' decision to go it alone songwriting and production-wise, set the band on a path of radical change. Furler stepped out from behind the drum kit to take the lead mike, Phillips moved from a percussion role into the timekeeper's seat behind the kit, and Joel, Davis, and

Frankenstein all had new roles to fulfill in this time of change.

From this upheaval came *Step Up to the Microphone*, the first fully contained Newsboys project ever, and one that showcased their new, tighter band and cutting edge version of modern pop. Once again, they

> James' departure, along with the remaining members' decision to go it alone songwriting and production-wise, set the band on a path of radical change.

headed out on the road with Furler initially fearing, then relishing his new spot out front, and audiences flocked to the shows.

Now comes *LoveLibertyDisco*, a project borne out of an abundance of songs the members brought to the table. It's a little more complex than past efforts in places, fluid string arrangements taking the space of what used to be bouncy synth parts or crunchy guitar licks. But it only serves to add another dimension to the Newsboys, one their lead singer/songwriter/producer is more than pleased to still be a part of.

PETER FURLER
Some Things Never Change

O ne favorite question for people who write about music and the people who play it is "What was the name of the first band you were in?"

For Peter Furler, the answer to that question is very simple, because he's still in that very first band. For Peter, the harder question comes when he's asked "Was it a Christian band?"

"Back where I was growing up, it wasn't a matter of being a Christian band

or not. It was more, 'Are you a good band or not?' I only remember one time

> "We've always been a band where we've made our mistakes, but there've only been a few times where we've looked back and been embarrassed by what we said or did."
>
> - Peter Furler

being asked to leave a pub because we were getting quite evangelical from

the stage," Peter says. "We've always been a band where we've made our mis-

takes, but there've only been a few times where we've looked back and been embarrassed by what we said or did."

There were those times in the early days, when the band first came to

America, when the living was pretty tough. Some people call those times the "salad days," but back then, Furler and his mates didn't even have enough money for that. "We lived on a dollar a day. We'd go to the convenience store, and they had a 99 cent hamburger, $1.06 with tax," Peter recalls now with a laugh.

Even as a kid, Peter Furler showed signs of the subtle charisma that helps the Newsboys entertain thousands of fans a night.

"We get that, and there'd be a tray with tomatoes and onions and pickles, and we'd pile the burger as high as we could, and that would be our meal for the day.

We befriended some other folks, and we'd go with them to buy food by the pound.

"It was pretty meager living, seven of us in one hotel room, shoving the double beds together and all piling on. It was definitely not the America that some guys thought it would be. Talking

For Peter, one good thing came out of the Newsboys' early days living in America— meeting his wife Summer.

about the early days is kinda weird, because I hardly remember them. I look at

the *Not Ashamed* days as the 'early days' because that's when this band started

taking its form."

But it wasn't

until 1998, more

than 10 years

> "It was pretty meager living, seven of us in one hotel room, shoving the double beds together and all piling on. It was definitely not the America that some guys thought it would be."
>
> - Peter Furler

after Furler pulled together the first version of this band, that he was forced to

make the career-changing move to being the Newsboys' frontman. He'd done vir-

tually everything else in the band: drummer, songwriter, producer, even auto

mechanic for the beaten-down fruit truck that served as their first touring vehicle back in Australia. But this was a whole new ballgame, one that Peter

admits he was not ready for.

<<>> Duncan Phillips on Peter Furler:

"Not only is Peter a great vocalist, but I've seen him develop as a pro-

ducer as well. He's really starting to develop his own 'flavor.'

"I'm starting to listen to how all the instruments sit sonically. A part I

play might feel great on its own, but when the melody is added, it clashes.

A shaker part might be played right on the money, but the accenting is

"It was such a shock that I don't think we felt anything, it was more a deer-in-the-headlights kind of surprise. It was never a matter of not continuing on,"

wrong, or it's too 'muddy.' I guess Peter has helped me to look beyond just drums and percussion and play for the song.

"I really admire his commitment to his craft because he never settles for less. The song's not going to be released until it's right, and that's good for all of us because it pushes us all to be our best."

Peter says. "And at the same time, we decided not to use Steve Taylor to produce

the record. We had about 40 concerts coming up, and we were making a record,

and it was one of those

> "...it was one of those things where you
> find out how good you can be when you're
> at your lowest point."
>
> - Peter Furler

things where you find out

how good you can be when

you're at your lowest point.

"There were some days when it didn't feel like it was going to be all right. At

the same time, there was kind of a peace about it."

The transition period that went on during the making of *Step Up to the

Microphone* and continued on through the tour for that album tested Peter's professional and personal will. "John was great on stage, and I felt like I didn't

want to let the guys down, but I'm not John James," Peter says. "It took a lot of

encouragement from the guys. They'd be very supportive, we'd come off stage

and they'd say, 'Man, you did great!' and I'd be 'This is not going to work. I'm a

better asset to this
band on the
drums.'"

Eventually,
though, Peter
began to feel

Even the Newsboys can be fans. Here they meet professional
motocross rider Greg Albertyn and his wife Amy for dinner in
Los Angeles.

comfortable being out front, as if everyone in this band he'd been working with since his teens was finally finding their way. "Jeff's always been a great keyboard player, Jody's always been a great guitar player. Phil was a terrible bass player," Peter laughs. "But he's worked so hard and now he's one of the best. Duncan sometimes doesn't realize the great thing he's doing, and that's playing it straight. So many drummers have taught themselves so many licks that they don't know how to keep a good beat.

"Phil and Jody both have stepped up more as vocalists, and especially with this new record, it's been about tapping into everybody's strengths."

For the young Peter Furler, the son of a missionary, the idea that he'd one day be the lead singer of a constantly on-the-go pop band might have been far-fetched, especially when his first memories of music involved a parked car. "I must have been under the age of 10, and I remember going out and sitting in Dad's car and listening to the radio. I'd put the keys in the ignition and turn the key half-way, so I could turn on the radio. I probably would have died from a heart attack had the car actually started," Peter says.

"I'd push the radio buttons and just scroll around. Then I remember being 13 years old or so and Dad bringing home a Walkman," Peter recalls. "From the duty-free shop he'd bring home the latest gadgets from where he'd been, like Papua New Guinea. I listened to the radio so much around that time that it got to the point that I would know what was coming up next. Just by the dead air, I could figure out what they'd play next."

And now, it's his songs that are getting played on the radio, and it's that process that appeals to the different musical facets of Peter Furler. " There are two sides of me, one side that would like to go down to New Orleans and just write music and lyrics and hand it to somebody and say, 'Go, make the music,'" he says. "The other side is that I just really enjoy the production work. I enjoy working with great people and getting a great drum sound and love putting things together. A lot of times those sides don't leave room for each other."

But, to Peter, the best part seems to be the relationships with the people he's had come into his circle of life, relationships that fulfill him on a personal and professional level. "It's great to be a man with these kinds of friends, rather than just be a group of guys with the same drive or ambitions," Peter says.

JODY DAVIS
In A Zone Of His Own

J ody Davis has found his favorite source of instant gratification. And it

has to do with instant film.

"My new love is my new Polaroid I-Zone camera, which takes these

little tiny pictures. Everybody who has seen it has just flipped over it," Jody

laughs. "It's all about immediate gratification. If you go into my studio, I've been documenting everything with this camera, and these little tiny pictures are

stuck all over the place. The studio is becoming a huge scrapbook."

Jody could probably fill a bunch of scrapbooks documenting his time with the Newsboys. Of the current members, he's logged the most

Still playing guitar? Check. Still sporting a mop of unruly hair? Check. The only thing missing from Jody Davis now is that oh-so-fashionable skinny tie.

time with the band, besides Peter, of course. And it seems he's the beginning of

the time-honored Newsboys tradition of throwing new members to the wolves as

quickly as possible.

"I hooked up with

the band after *Not*

> And it seems he's the beginning of the time-honored Newsboys tradition of throwing new members to the wolves as quickly as possible.

Ashamed came out, because they didn't really have a guitar player at the time,"

Jody says. "They hired me to go out with them for a few weeks and I guess I just

never left."

As the Newsboys' second-in-seniority, he's not only seen several people

come and go from the band, he's also seen the group pass through a number of different musical styles. Which doesn't seem to bother him at all. "We're not

really interested in getting stuck doing one kind of thing. We try to reinvent

<<>> Peter Furler on Jody Davis:

"I remember one time Jody coming up to me and saying, 'You don't have to be John James. Be who you are and develop it.' It was a good thing for me to hear.

"Now that I'm out front, and Jody and Phil are locked in with what I'm doing vocally, we've kinda got that Fleetwood Mac thing going on. I guess that would make Jody Lindsay Buckingham because Phil would have to be Stevie Nicks.

ourselves every record, and try to do something that's interesting and fresh to

us," Jody says. "Our live thing has always been a straight-up, rock 'n roll kind of

"Jody is definitely right there, every bit as talented as a guy like Lindsay Buckingham, and nobody really knows it.

"The difference with Jody is that he's not really a self-promoter. He doesn't have many massive ambitions, he loves the simple life, which makes him a great guy to have in the band. He does what he does, and he does it extremely well."

thing anyway, so as soon as the record's done, the songs take on the life that they're supposed to take on."

They're so proud. Jody with his parents John and Devera Davis.

But it's the success of live shows as well other trappings of the music business that causes some people to view members of a rock band as something other than just plain folks, people who take each breath the same way everyone else does. It's a notion Jody wants to at least attempt to dispel.

"The biggest downside is that people stop looking at you as being a normal person. I can't tell you how many people we come across who think, 'You're doing well, you must be some kind of super Christians,'" he says. "You know what? We

> "The biggest downside is that people stop looking at you as being a normal person."
> - Jody Davis

are in no way better off than anybody else when it comes to that. We have our problems and our struggles we deal with, everybody does. Even Billy Graham has those things he deals with. But it's hard to let people know that.

"I think in a lot of ways it's a problem of the whole church because people are so concerned with keeping up their appearances and worried about being bad examples. But in all reality, a bad example is somebody who thinks they've got it all together, but really, nobody does," Jody continues. "What you're doing then is setting a false example, and it's a lie. It's much better to be real, and it's been more and more difficult the more success we've had to convince folks that we're real people.

"We're just a bunch of musicians. Musicians are usually the last guys you want to look up to. There are a lot of people out in the world doing great, great things. We're just playing music."

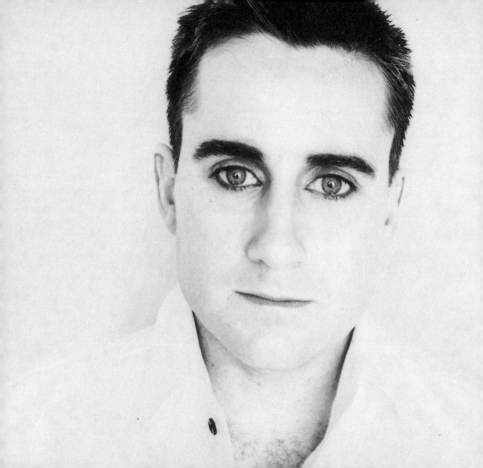

DUNCAN PHILLIPS
Sticking With It

As far as any myths Duncan Phillips would like to dispel, those would deal with growing up in Australia versus growing up in America. He's here to tell you it wasn't necessarily the outback adventure some folks might like to think it was.

"I just went to school like everyone else," Duncan says. "It was

Even at a young age, Duncan Phillips showed flashes of the sartorial sharpness he exudes today. Pictured are: Duncan (at top), and his siblings Melissa, Tim and Gita.

pretty much a normal childhood, just on the other side of the world!"

It was in that school where young Mr. Phillips first got a taste of the instruments that would define his life. "Back in elementary school, we used to have an assembly before class. We used to have to line up and listen to the principal tell what was going to happen that day or whatever, and as we went into our classes, we had to kind of march into our classrooms," Duncan says. "But to march, of course, we needed a marching band. So that was my first taste of playing the drums, which I thought were pretty cool.

"But to march, of course, we needed a marching band. So that was my first taste of playing the drums, which I thought were pretty cool."
                                                            - Duncan Phillips

"When I went into high school, I got into keyboards as well as drums, and was trained classically on the piano for several years, not that you'd know it now," he laughs.

NEWSBOYS

It's time, once again, to play that internationally famous game, "Where's Duncan?" Answer: He's the front row bowl cut holding the sign.

Although Jody's been in the band longer, Duncan's relationship with

Peter goes back to the very earliest days of the Newsboys. "When I was 21 or 22, I met Peter at church. He and I used to hang out and go surfing. We just formed a friendship, but it was a pretty competitive friendship because at the time I was in another rock band and he was just starting the Newsboys," Duncan says. "If anybody wanted a band to come play at their church or youth group, they'd call our band, and then along come these punks, the Newsboys! They were invading our turf, so I had to check these guys out. For a few years, we had this kind of friendly rivalry between our bands, and that's where I got to know Peter."

As seems to be the case with the Newsboys, fate intervened when they were in need of a new member. "In '93, I was over here playing in a band on the West Coast, and came over to Nashville to pick up some gear. I was only

here for a few weeks, and I didn't run into Pete, but ran into one of his

<<>> Phil Joel on Duncan Phillips

"You probably couldn't find two more opposite human beings on the
planet to be in the same rhythm section. And that makes it fun.

"He's a builder, so he's a very practical thinking kind of guy. I'll forget
to tie my shoes if somebody doesn't remind me. I think it makes for good
music, because you've got the push and pull.

"We often rub musically, which can be good. He's usually got an idea
about a rhythm and how I should play it, and I've got a different idea
about how he should play it, and usually we'll meet in the middle and

friends at church who saw me there," Duncan says. "The Newsboys' keyboard player had just left, and this guy told Pete, 'Why don't you give

come up with something quite fresh.

"It was hard when Peter stepped out front, because we think a lot alike musically. I had gotten kind of spoiled having my first drummer think like me. Duncan plays differently, so I had to rethink how I played, which has been quite exciting for me.

"That and he's got great taste. Very expensive taste. An extremely hygienic human being, very pressed, always starched, which might be odd for a drummer."

Duncan a call? He's over here now.' Peter was like, 'No way!' So we got in

contact, and I went in to audition.

"I was there to audition for the keyboard slot, but there were a couple

of tracks where Pete was out front singing lead vocals, so I jumped behind

the kit. I think he audi-

> "There's a big difference between playing
> drums and being the drummer. It was scary,
> it was exciting, and it was a lot of work."
> - Duncan Phillips

tioned three or four guys,

but I was the only one who

could play both keys and drums, plus there was the Australian connection."

And then there's the typical trial by fire. "My first show was at

Creation '93 in front of 60,000 people or so, and I had two days to learn

DUNCAN PHILLIPS: **Sticking With It**

Should this music thing not work out, Duncan seems to have quite a gift for motivational speaking.

the songs. No pressure there," Duncan says. "For a couple of days there I was sweating bullets, trying to grind these songs into my head, and not think about being in front of a sea of people a few days later."

When Peter left the drum kit and moved out front for good, Duncan was the member whose role changed the most. "There's a big difference between playing drums and being the drummer. It was scary, it was exciting, and it was a lot of work. I went in for weeks and just practiced and practiced and practiced, because my chops weren't there. I hadn't been a drummer in a band for quite a few years, and I felt like I had pretty big shoes to fill, because Pete had been playing drums in the Newsboys forever," Duncan says. "It was almost like I had to learn the songs again in my head. You think you know all the other parts, but when you have to relearn how things start and stop, where to play hard and where to play soft, it can be a pretty daunting experience."

It's been in the growth and change, the good times and the bad, that Duncan sees where the strength of the unit the Newsboys have become has emerged. "We started off as a bunch of young guys who wanted to play music. And it's really as God has molded us over the years that we've discovered what's in our hearts. That's been great to watch."

NEWSBOYS

Photo Gallery

It doesn't matter whether they're on stage or on motorbikes—the Newsboys wring every drop out of their high-octane lives. Step inside to see how they got from "then and there" to here and now.

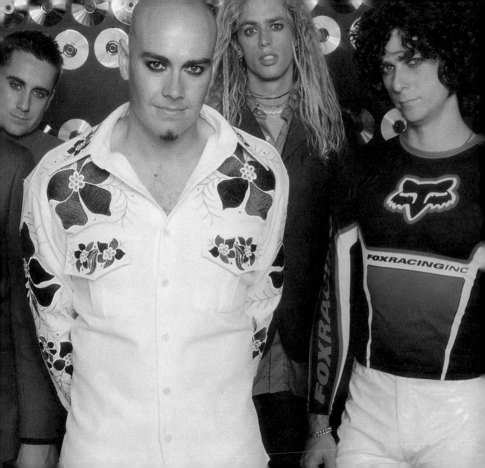

The young Newsboys at their very first video shoot, which chronicled the song "Simple Man."

Haven't we seen this pose before? Filming the "Take Me To Your Leader" video.

The Newsboys took to the road outside Los Angeles for the video shoot for "Entertaining Angels." They're seen here with director Eden and producer Joel Newman.

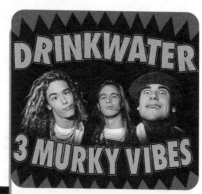

Believe it or not, there was a musical life before the Newsboys for Phil Joel, seen here on an ultra-rare Drinkwater album cover.

Phil's not the only famous face in the Joel household. Wife Heather is a co-host on CMT's "Hit Trip" program.

When they're not all storming the stage together, the members of the Newsboys all indulge in their favorite group activity, motocross riding. Here the musical daredevils take to the Baja desert in Mexico.

Cleans up nice, doesn't he? The newly wed couple says their farewells.

The bandmates (and wives) who travel together, stay together: Jody and Erika Davis and Duncan and Breon Phillips meet Venice, Italy.

The Phillips clan at Christmastime.

Early on, Jeff showed signs of preferring alternative modes of transportation. Then it was a wooden horse, now it's a tour bus.

What is it with this kid and bikes?

Young Jeff with his parents, John and Sandy, and sister Becky.

Jody wasn't always the guitar hero we've come to know. In his very first band at age 13, he played mandolin. That'd explain the outfits.

1986. Enough said.

Apparently Jody and Jeff didn't listen when their moms told them not to play in traffic. Especially traffic in London.

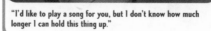

"I'd like to play a song for you, but I don't know how much longer I can hold this thing up."

JEFF FRANKENSTEIN
Hitting The Ground Running

The thinking would normally go this way: Jeff Frankenstein, the youngest member and keyboard player of the Newsboys, a band known for its use of technology in the record making process—this guy has to be tricked out in all the latest, bleeding edge music making gadgetry, right?

"85...86...87...88...Yep, they're all here."

Wrong.

"I did all the sequencing for this record on a 1983 Atari that I just can't seem to get rid of," Jeff says. "It works perfectly, it's never crashed on me, and there's a company in Germany that's still writing new software for it."

Well, that blows that theory. Then again, Jeff has become somewhat known for drawing inspiration from weird places.

After all, here's a guy who grew up in Detroit, a city fairly reeking with musical history, what with Motown and all of its associated legends. So,

you'd expect the primary driving force behind a kid interested in keyboards

would be somebody like Stevie

Wonder, right?

> Then again, Jeff has become somewhat known for drawing inspiration from weird places.

Yes, maybe so, but how about

Liberace?

"My grandparents lived about a block from us when I was growing up,

and my grandfather had this old, crusty Wurlitzer organ in the house. He

loved music, too, and he had all these old Big Band records, Benny Goodman

and those guys," Jeff remembers. "He had this Liberace songbook...you know, the books that just had the chord charts in them? He'd keep this

book in the bench by the organ, and we'd mess around playing these songs

out of this songbook. My grandma and grandpa would come in, and I'd play

all these old songs for them.

> "He'd just let me come over and jam on that organ for hours and hours, and that really started it."
> - Jeff Frankenstein

"He saw that love of music in me, but he didn't really push me toward it. He'd just let me come over and jam on that organ for hours and hours, and that really started it."

That love for music continued on through his school years, through

church bands and high school groups, and even manifested itself much the way his future bandmate Furler's did halfway around the world. "I remember

going to bed at night and putting on a little set of headphones and listening

to music all night. I'd flip through all the stations in Detroit just to hear

what was playing. I loved doing that, because it was my own little time to

check out what was going on," Jeff says.

And, like many other of his future
bandmates, his introduction to the
band was all about diving in head
first. The summer after Jeff gradu-
ated high school, he met Peter at a

For young Frankenstein, climbing trees was far
less dangerous than his early days with the
Newsboys.

Newsboys show. The two hit it off, finding common ground in talking about

a keyboard they had both just bought. Almost a year later, Jeff got a call

from Furler, telling him the keyboard slot in the band was open and asking if

 <<>> **Jody Davis on Jeff Frankenstein:**

"When he first got in the band, he was very young, very green. We

used to torment him unmercifully. He'd hold the curtain on his bunk closed

for an hour before going to sleep because there was no telling what was

going to happen. He spent those first few months just scared to death.

"I think he brings a lot of great things to the band musically. He's got he'd like to try out.

"I drove out that weekend to meet the guys. Realize, I hadn't seen
them in over a year, and Jody had joined the band since then, but I didn't

a great pop sensibility to him, he's got a good sense about what's cool
and what isn't. He's always coming up with interesting stuff.

"We've been roommates a lot of the time on the road, so we have a
lot of fun together. But he's always been a real mature guy for his age,
and he's got a great walk with the Lord."

realize he was part of the band until he went on stage. He was just working as part of the crew like everybody else," Jeff says. "They pull me in, and I'm working all day with these guys, so it comes time for sound check, and they say, 'Well, why don't you set up and just play along?'

"We went through these songs, one after another, and they were diggin' it. They come up to me afterwards and say, 'So...do you want to play tonight?' It was only later that I found out that was typical Newsboys' style, throw somebody in and see what he's got," Jeff recalls. "Here I am, I don't even know all the guys in the band's names, none of them know mine, and I'm onstage that night. I play the show that night, and afterwards, they're like, 'Do you want to come out next week in Indianapolis?' I go home and tell my parents, 'Well, I played with them,' and the next day I dropped out of college.

> "I just left it all behind: friends, family, 20 years of my life, just with a desire to go for it."
>
> — Jeff Frankenstein

"I spent the next two days making preparations, and loaded up my little white Cavalier with everything I owned and drove to Nashville, not knowing where I was gonna live. I just left it all behind: friends, family, 20 years of my life, just with a desire to go for it. I drove down to Nashville and I've pretty much been truckin' ever since."

PHIL JOEL
Making It Up As He Goes

When you're the last guy to join a band, you spend a lot of time just trying to prove yourself. In Phil Joel's case, he spent a lot of time just proving he could play the instrument he'd been hired to play.

That's not to say Phil wasn't a musician. In fact, he'd given up

You *can* go home again: Jeff and Heather Joel visiting Jeff's grandfather in New Zealand.

PHIL JOEL: Making It Up As He Goes

what he thought was going to be his profession—hairdressing—after a

four-year apprenticeship, because Drinkwater, the band in which he was a

guitarist, songwriter, and vocalist, was starting to have a good bit of suc-

cess in their native

New Zealand.

It's just that he

wasn't entirely truth-

> "They asked if I could play bass, and I immediately said, 'Sure I can play the bass.' How hard can it be? I can play a guitar with six strings—four big fat strings should be a cinch."
> - Phil Joel

ful when Peter Furler, who had seen Joel perform when Drinkwater

opened for Newsboys on a New Zealand tour, called asking if he wanted

to be the Newsboys' bass player. "They asked if I could play bass, and I immediately said, 'Sure I can play the bass.' How hard can it be?' I can

play a guitar with six strings—four big fat strings should be a cinch."

<<>> **Jeff Frankenstein on Phil Joel:**

"Phil is a guy who is overflowing with natural talent. He emanates it. He's

the kind of guy who has it, but sometimes needs other people in the band to

help harness it.

"I look at his role in the band as an extremely important one. He's very out-

going, very friendly, very generous, and has a heart for the Lord like very few

people I've met.

"In all my conversations with Phil about spiritual things, he's always had

PHIL JOEL: Making It Up As He Goes

"I quickly swapped one of my guitars for a bass, and the next day,

I'm on a plane, flying to Los Angeles, listening to a Newsboys record and

something to say that has helped mold me and change my perspective on things.

"Phil's the kind of guy who really has a heart for people who are down and

out or suffering. He's a guy who's really longing to have a heart like Jesus. He's

always really open and wears his heart on his sleeve, but it's cool because you

know it's the real deal. He's a world-class vocalist, and has trained himself to be

a great bass player. I can't think of another guy I'd want to hold down the bass

slot in this band."

trying to figure out how to play these bass lines," he continues. "I tried

really hard to be a bass player, to play the bass the way I thought a real

bass player would

play. We were in a

rehearsal room, and I

> "I was adopted, so I had a bunch of questions as to why I was like I was and why the rest of my family were the way they were."
>
> - Phil Joel

was trying my hardest, and I could see everybody thinking, 'What have

we done? We put this guy on a plane and here he is and he can't play!'

"I finally just threw up my hands and said, 'Do you guys mind if I play

with a pick?' So I grabbed a pick and started playing, and guys started

smiling so I thought, 'Well, I must be doing something right.' That was the

PHIL JOEL: Making It Up As He Goes

The younger Phil Joel, shortly after his last real haircut.

turning point, even though I thought that playing bass with a pick was evil, that it was a bad thing to do. But it turns out to be the best thing I could have done."

Let's back up for just a second, though. Here's a young man who had to make a career choice between hairdressing and being a musician, two things you wouldn't mentally associate with the rough 'n tumble image of New Zealand, right?

Turns out Phil's talents were instilled in him before he was even born.

"I was adopted, so I had a bunch of questions as to why I was like

I was and why the rest of my family were the way they were. All of the

> "I don't know if it's so much the band has changed since I've been in it—it's more that the band has changed me."
>
> - Phil Joel

rest of the members of my family are very practical-minded people who

love to work on cars. And I never really fit in with my father and brothers

out there in the garage working on cars," Phil says. "I went through the phases, like any other kid, of wanting to be a fireman or a truck driver, but it was at 13, when I took my first guitar lesson, that I knew, 'This is it. Now it all makes sense to me.'

"Later on, I met my birth mother and found out a little more about my birth parents. She was a wig maker, which explains the hairdressing thing, and he was a musician, which explains the rest. I had fulfilled my destiny without even trying," he claims.

These days, he's more than proven himself to his bandmates, developing a songwriting relationship with Furler that provides the thrust of the band's new material. He's a focal point on stage, his long blond locks swirling around while he spins around on one foot playing the instrument he wasn't so sure he could master. And while he hasn't been around for all of the band's variations, he can see where important changes have taken place.

"I don't know if it's so much the band has changed since I've been in it—it's more that the band has changed me. I've never seen or been in a band that's as close as we are, especially one that has five such different people. We've all got respect for each other, and just huge, huge friend-ships," Phil says. "Those insecurities about bringing up songs or diving in with ideas, they're all gone now. We know each other, we like each other, we respect each other enough to know that if there's a differing view-

point, it's still gonna be cool."

Newsboys, back stage with the legendary Tony Bennett

STILL CRAZY AFTER ALL THESE YEARS

You think a Newsboys show is frenetic and high-energy? You should see what these guys do to relax.

Several years ago, it was a full-bore embracing of the paintball craze, as Jeff Frankenstein learned in his early days with the band. "You'd go into a fast-food joint and these guys were packing their paintball pistols. Everybody was living in paranoia, because you'd be eating, and someone would get up to leave and you'd start thinking to yourself, 'I'm gonna go outside and just get pelted,'" Jeff says. "There were wars every night, everybody had a pistol in their bunk on the bus, bus drivers gettin' shot at point blank range, and here I am, a 20-year-old kid, thrown right into the middle of this lunacy."

"So we've definitely gotten a lot nicer to each other over the years, but we've definitely gotten more psycho, because everybody's now into dirtbikes," Jeff continues. "We've taken trips down to Mexico and to Baja California, gotten lost in the desert. We definitely tap into that adventurous spirit, it's what keeps the band going."

"I enjoy getting back to nothing," Peter says. "You've pretty much just got a backpack and you just ride. I had been a surfer all my life until we hit the road, and motocross has kinda taken the place of that over the past six or seven years."

> "I enjoy getting back to nothing. You've pretty much just got a backpack and you just ride. I had been a surfer all my life until we hit the road, and motocross has kinda taken the place of that over the past six or seven years."
>
> - Peter Furler

Getting back to nothing can be a needed experience, especially when the rigors, or more precisely the repetition, of the road begin to wear on your body, or more precisely your digestive system. "I remember there were a few months there where we got lasagna at every meal, to the point where we had to put it into our contract rider 'No lasagna,'" Duncan says. "And we know that these good people look at the 30 or 40 guys they have to feed, and think about what they can mass produce, and go 'Aha! Lasagna!' But when you have it for three months straight, it kind of loses its appeal. So that's why the clause is there, and I don't think it's ever coming out."

"Lasagna and motorcycles are why we have a legion of people praying for our safety," Duncan laughs.

TEAMWORK

To a man, the members of the Newsboys stress the importance of the way they function as a unit. They all agree it's taken a long time, and it's just now starting to really manifest itself in their output.

"I think we all have a part in the decision making process, and we're all very close with our manager Wes Campbell, so it's really six guys sitting down and saying, 'Here's the issue, how do we resolve it?' It's not like you do that with everything, but it's good to have that input," Duncan says.

With their varied backgrounds and interests, especially musically, that input makes for some very interesting opinions about the music they're making. "Everybody dabbles in something else in this band," Jody says. "Everybody plays a little guitar, everybody plays a little keyboard, everybody plays some drums, so we all put our two cents in about every part."

And if there's ever a time when one guy starts indulging in a "rock star moment," he's got four other guys right there to bring him back down to reality in a hurry. "We hear the cheers and yes, we're a little flattered by it, but at the same time, we don't really understand it because we get back on the bus and we all know how crusty we all are. It's like, 'If they only knew...'" Jeff says.

In the long run, though, the success can be attributed to their common goal of seeking the will of their ultimate team member, God. "It sounds like a trite answer, but it's always been about seeking first the kingdom of God. Individually and corporately, and hopefully bringing a few fans, even the kicking and screaming ones, along as well," Phil says. "That's pretty much the long and short of it. Part of that is that we should always be striving to improve: as human beings, as musicians, as husbands, as men of God, as fathers. If we're not improving, then we need to take a good long look at why we're not and try to rectify that."

IN THE END

What does the future hold for the Newsboys? Well, if the past is any indication, they'll be touring...a lot. And they'll continue to make music based on what God puts on their hearts. "We don't have goals of world domination or hits on the charts. We've seen what that has done for other bands. We're so blessed to be in the position we're in," Peter says.

No, for the Newsboys, it's more about using the position they're in, the platform they've been given, to try to make a difference on a more human level. "It's the day-by-day stuff: helping the poor, feeding the hungry," Jeff says. "It wouldn't surprise me to find out that pulling someone off the street one day to help with catering at a show led to something amazing and meant more than 90% of the other stuff we do. We just do what we do and hope God can use it."

"What we're trying to do is just be really true in our own hearts and with what we feel like God has put us here to do. Being musicians and doing this sort of thing is in our blood and in our make-up. So we're just trying to be that. We try to write as a by-product of what is in our hearts, and we're always hoping and praying that those things will be glorifying to God," Jody says. "The truth of the

matter is, we're not trying to be big missionaries to teenagers, we're just writing

music and playing music out of our own personal experiences and what moves us.

We just hope it'll move other people as well."

Who knew what could grow out of lunchtime on the other side of the world?

Wes Campbell, Newsboys manager:

"I first met Peter and The Newsboys in Broadbeach, Queensland, Australia, on a late Friday afternoon. I was told by Duncan Phillips, Peter's main drumming rival on the Sunshine Coast, that there was a young band he knew, still practicing in the drummer's garage, that showed potential and were worth checking out. So I booked them for my music club. Being one of their very first gigs, the 'boys were all too eager to drive the 200 miles from Mooloolaba to Broadbeach to play.

"Although I didn't realize it then, that night was to change the course of my life. Before I heard a single note of music, I knew these guys were different. My standard contract with bands had two choices: $300.00 cash, or I spend the

$300.00 hiring a great sound system and we all go eat at Burger King at the end of the night. The Newsboys were the first band ever to choose the King, and I knew they had a vision. After being blown away by their concert that night, I shared that vision too.

"So I packed up my family in a suitcase and moved to the U.S.A., beginning an 11 year journey (and counting!) that has made The Newsboys one of the biggest bands in Christian music. More importantly, it has taken us to almost every city on almost every continent in the world, hopefully touching lives, as God has touched ours."

Peter Furler on *Read All About It*: <<>>

We recorded this record in 6 days in a studio in West Orange, New Jersey. It was the band's first trip to the USA, our first time to see snow, freeways, Cadillacs, and 6-inch televisions.

Peter Furler on *Hell Is For Wimps*: <<>>

We recorded this record in Atlanta, Georgia, and off this record we shot our first ever "real" video for the song "Simple Man."

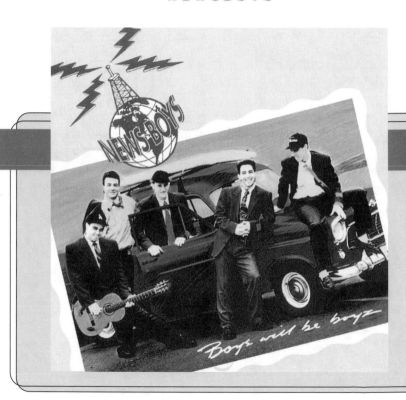

Peter Furler on *Boys Will Be Boyz*: <<>>

This CD was recorded in a studio just off the
Gold Coast (Queensland, Australia). The whole
band caught chicken pox off each other and
that's all I have to say about that.

Peter Furler on *Not Ashamed*: <<>>

This record to me feels like our first "real" record. It was the first time we felt like we had some control over our music and it was the start of a wonderful friendship with Steve Taylor.

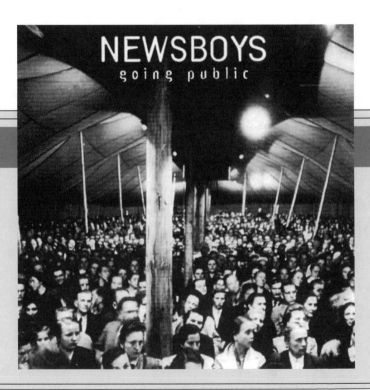

Peter Furler on *Going Public*: <<>>

We had 9 songs recorded for this CD (time was running out as usual) so we quickly had to write one more—we came up with a little song called "Shine."

Peter Furler on *Take Me To Your Leader*: <<>>

We were recording this record on our 'off' days on the *Going Public* tour, so we recorded parts of this album in Hollywood, Miami, Nashville, Burbank, and featured for the first time our fans in Milwaukee, Wisconsin, Stillwater, Oklahoma, and Ottumwa, Iowa, singing on the song "Breakfast."

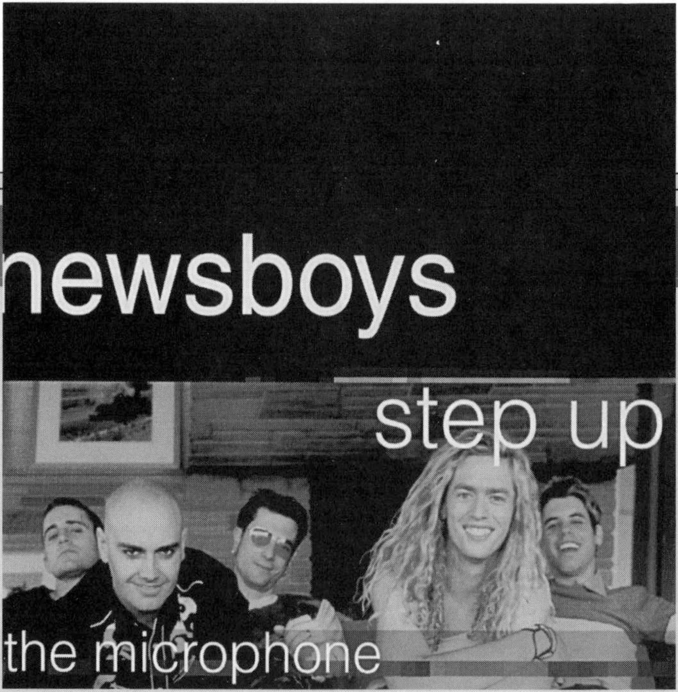
newsboys
step up
the microphone

Peter Furler on *Step Up To The Microphone*: <<>>

We recorded and mixed this CD in a room in my house. I remember the string quartet scratched up my wood floors with their music stands, etc.—that's all I have say about that also!

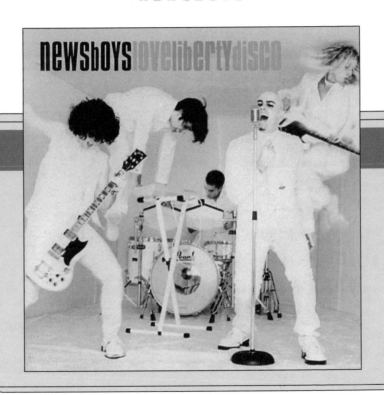

Peter Furler on *LoveLibertyDisco*: <<>>

This CD was recorded back at a studio called "the White House" (where we recorded some of *Take Me To Your Leader*). It is my favorite so far—the most enjoyable and positive time for us as friends both creatively and spiritually, but I really think the best is yet to come.

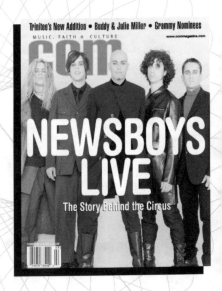